LINUX

Beginner's Crash Course

Linux for Beginner's Guide to Linux Command Line, Linux System & Linux Commands

not engaging in the rendering of legal, financial, medical or professional advice.

By reading this document, the reader agrees that under no circumstances are we responsible for any losses, direct or indirect, which are incurred as a result of the use of information contained within this document, including, but not limited to, —errors, omissions, or inaccuracies.

Table of Contents

Introduction

Linux, once thought of as an underdog operating system, which remained in obscurity overshadowed by the mighty Windows, has been winning accolades among software developers, businesses and PC users in recent times. This UNIX variant, whose regular users were once only geeks and nerds, is gaining immense popularity among home computer users too.

Linux gained popularity among software developers as it is free of charge and runs on different platforms. Linux has been amassing a dedicated audience and has attracted different groups of people as follows:

- People who are acquainted with Unix and interested in running it on personal computers

- People who are interested in experimenting with the principles of operating systems

- People who want an operating system which gives them maximum control

- People who are not satisfied with Microsoft

Managing Linux is harder, when compared to Windows, yet Linux is more flexible and has more configuration options.

Businesses seem to be conquering their irrational suspicion of Linux and are adapting Linux for most of their business applications. Linux is free and open source and hence the companies need not worry about licensing while adapting it to develop their business applications. That makes it a pretty tempting proposition.

Chapter 1:
Linux-Overview

If you are a computer programmer, in all probability, you will know about LINUX. Maybe you have read about Linux somewhere, or perhaps one of your friends might have told you. Linux is interesting. The more you learn about LINUX, the more interesting questions you'll have about it.

What is LINUX?

In general, there are two types of PC users; the ones who look at the computer as an amazing tool with which they can do cool stuff like browsing, playing, watch movies, playing music, etc. They might even have knowledge about the hardware components like RAM, processors, audio and video cards, graphic cards etc. For most PC users, it is not important or interesting for them to know about the complexity behind these simple processes. They open a browser, type the address and somehow the website opens. They are not interested in knowing how it happens.

Then there are the second set of people who are actually interested on knowing how things work internally. Almost everyone considers an operating system as additional software. It is not. An operating system, just like any other hardware component, is an important part of a computer. When needed, the operating system can be upgraded or swapped for a better performing operating system or for a more suited replacement.

Advantages of LINUX

Whenever you talk about Linux, you have probably heard people seemingly exaggerating about how awesome it is. In fact, it is true. The main advantages of Linux over other operating systems include the following:

Crash Free:

LINUX is a crash free operating system. When using Linux, no user experiences freezing of the cursor on the screen, sudden system crashes, error messages that won't go unless you reboot your system etc. The programs or applications that run on the LINUX operating system might crash but the operating system will be functioning and the application cannot take it down when it crashes. In LINUX, unlike other operating systems, you can simply clean up after the program crash and carry on. The crash free nature of LINUX is a very reliable when dealing with operations like space research, nuclear research, etc. where you cannot risk system crashes which might result in huge expenses being incurred.

Security:

The next advantage of LINUX is its security. The security of the LINUX operating system is far more secure compared to other operating systems like Windows, which has many security flaws. The reason for such security of the LINUX operating system is because of the years of extensive computer science research that has gone into it. In Linux, if you do not have the appropriate permissions, you will not be allowed to access a particular piece of hardware or a particular folder in the system. In clinics, privacy can be set to individual owners who can only access their own files. The root user will have access over the complete system and he can limit user access to other users.

Free and **Shareable**:

LINUX is a free operating system, which is another major benefit for users working on LINUX. After the installation of the operating system, the latest updates will be downloaded free of charge. When a new version of the operating system is available, you can simply replace it with your current version and can use it. In fact, you can actually download any version of Linux and use it. As it is free software, it can be shared among a group of people. Default applications like image viewers, default music player, image editors, etc. can all be shared among friends or other people who like it. This is not possible with the Windows or other operating systems and somehow copying these kinds of applications and sharing them with others will make you a software pirate. That is not the case with the LINUX operating system. With LINUX, it is completely legal to share software between different users. And the sharing is actually encouraged with LINUX.

Compatibility:

The other benefit of using the LINUX operating system is that it can work even with older hardware without needing a high performance, cutting edge PC like other operating systems that need the latest configurations for running their latest operating system. For example, the new version of Windows will need good hardware configuration for it to run. The Linux operating system can even work on old hardware without this same problem. So, you don't need to buy high-performance hardware if you wish to work with LINUX. You can see the difference for yourself when you install the LINUX operating system and any other operating system on the same hardware.

The LINUX operating system will work faster and better when compared to other operating systems like windows, which are power hungry. The LINUX group encourages users to recycle and reuse hardware components by making the most of the given hardware. You can actually bring an old computer system back to life by installing LINUX on it and can even give it to a friend or family member who doesn't own a PC. That's got to make sense.

Flexibility:

The LINUX operating system is extremely flexible. With the LINUX operating system, you can turn your old hardware into a web server or any other task like that. Linux can work on almost 60% of computers, which makes the Internet work. With Linux, it is possible to convert your old PC system into an email server, web server or even into a firewall and can connect it to the broadband Internet connection. Doing the same tasks using other operating systems would cost you a fortune not to mention that you will need a high-performance PC system.

The LINUX community:

We have seen the important features of Linux, like its crash-free nature, security, compatibility and flexibility. But that is not all. The best feature of using Linux is the Linux community. LINUX is not just a computer operating system, there is more to it. When you start using LINUX, you become a part of this huge community (whether you like it or not) called the Linux community that is spread across the globe. Being a part of the Linux community has its own advantages. One such benefit of being a member is that you are never far from finding a solution for whatever problem you may have. Most of the people in this community encourage using Linux and help others to solve their problems by providing solutions for them. Whenever a new member joins the Linux community, he will be termed as a 'newbie.' It sounds derisory, but it is a good opportunity for him to talk with other professional Linux programmers. All these professional LINUX programmers believe that knowledge should be shared freely and help other people learn LINUX. When someone advertises his status as a newbie, people will make time to help him because, after all, those professionals were once newbies as well.

Overview

An operating system can be considered as an interface or as an intermediary between the computer hardware and the users. Operating systems provide users with an environment that will allow them to execute different programs efficiently and conveniently. Technically speaking, an operating system is nothing but software that manages the hardware on which it is being run. An operating system is responsible for the allocation of services and resources like processors, memory, devices and information. The LINUX is one such operating system.

Definition

As previously stated, an operating system is a program, which acts as an interface between the user and the computer hardware and controls the execution of all kinds of programs.

The important functions of any operating system are given below:

- Memory Management

- Device Management

- Processor Management

- Security

- File Management

- Control over system performance

- Error detecting aids

- Job accounting

- Coordination between other software and users

Memory Management

Management is nothing but managing the main memory or the primary memory. Memory can be considered as a very large array of bytes or words that has an address of its own.

The main memory provides the CUP with direct access and faster storage. So if you want to execute a program, it should be stored in the main memory of the computer. Every operating system, including the LINUX operating system, performs the following memory management activities.

- Keeping a track of the main memory. This includes keeping track of used and unused memory. In case of used memory, it will keep a track of the users using it.

- Operating system will decide to allocate memory for different processes in case of multiprogramming.

- It also allocates memory whenever a certain process requests extra memory.

- Operating systems also take care of the memory de-allocation when a particular process is terminated or when it no longer needs memory.

Processor Management

In a multiprogramming environment, the operating system is the program that decides the processor allocation time for each process. For processor management, every operating system will perform the following activities:

- Keeping track of process status and processor status. The traffic controller is the program that takes care of this.

- The processor management is responsible for allocating the processor to a given process

- The operating system's processor management is responsible for the allocation of the processor when it is not required.

Device Management

The devices communicate with each other using their own drivers. The OS is responsible for this communication. An operating system's device manager performs the following activities:

- Keeping a track on all the available devices. The I/O controller is the program responsible for performing this task.

- The device manager is the manager that decides the allocation of a particular device to process. It is also responsible for the allocation of time for which the process needs the device.

- It efficiently allocates devices to processes.

- De-allocation is also taken care by the device management.

File Management

For easy usage and navigation, a file system will be organized into directories. Files and other directions will be stored in these directories. The operating system performs the following file management activities:

- It keeps track of the status, uses, location, information etc. The file system is a collective of these facilities.

- The operating systems file management is the program that decides the allocation of resources.

- This will also decide who gets to use the resources.

- Keeps track of information, location, uses, status etc. The collective facilities are controlled within this file management system.

- De-allocation of resources is taken care by the file management.

Other Important Activities

Here are few of the important activities that are performed by an operating system.

- **Security** - By using a password or other such similar technique, the operating system will prevent any unauthorized access to data and programs.

- **Control over system performance** - An operating system will have control over the system performance by recording the delays sent by the service as a request and the response given by the system.

- **Job accounting** - The operating system is responsible for keeping track of the resources and time used by different users on various jobs.

- **Error detecting aids** - For error detection, the operating system will produce places, error messages, dumps and a few other errors detecting and debugging aids.

- **Coordination between other software and users** - The operating system takes care of the coordination and assignment of assemblers, compilers, interpreters and any other software to other users who use the computer system.

Types of Operating Systems

Operating systems have been in use from the very first generation of computers. Over this period of time, the operating systems continuously evolve. Here are a few of the important operating systems that are used commonly.

Batch operating system

When using a batch operating system, the users and the computer will not interact directly. Every job that a user prepares will be made into an off-line device similar to punch cards and it will be submitted to the computer operator. For better performance and speed, these jobs will be batched together and made into a group. The computer will run this group all at once together with all the jobs. The programmers will leave their programs to the operator and the operators will sort of these programs (depending on their type) into batches that have similar requirements. Though this is a good practice, the batch operating system has its own disadvantages. They are:

- There will be no interaction between the job and the user.

- For most of the time, the CPU will be left idle. This is because of the difference in speeds between the CPU and the mechanical I/O devices. The mechanical devices are obviously slower than a CPU.

- With batch operating systems, it will be difficult to provide the properties desired.

Time-sharing operating systems

Timesharing is a technique where various terminals can be located on a particular computer system that can be used at the same time. Multitasking or time sharing is a multiprogramming logical extension. The simultaneous sharing of the processor time among different users is called time-sharing. The main difference between the time sharing systems and the multiprogrammed batch system is that the multiprogramming batch system looks for maximizing the processor efficiency whereas minimizing the response time is the main objective for time sharing systems.

Here, jobs will be frequent, can switch and be executed by the processor, meaning that the users can get immediate responses. Let us take a transaction processing for example where the processor will execute the programs in the quantum of computation or in a short burst. The response time for every user at the most is a few seconds.

Every operating system will use the multiprogramming and scheduling of the CPU and provides them with a small fraction of time. The computer systems that were primarily designed for running as batch sharing systems have all later been modified into time sharing systems.

Advantages and disadvantages of time-sharing operating systems:

The following are the advantages of the timesharing operating systems:

- Timesharing operating systems provide the users with quick responses.

- Timesharing operating systems avoid software duplication.

- The CPU idle time in time sharing operating systems is reduced.

The following are the disadvantages of using time sharing operating system:

- There is a reliability problem with the timesharing operating system.

- With the timesharing operating systems, the integrity and security of the data and use your programs might be at risk.

- Problem with reliability.

Distributed operating System

The distributed operating system deals with multiple users and multiple real-time applications that are using multiple CPUs. Efficiency of the job being performed will be increased as the data processing tasks will be distributed among different processors accordingly.

Processes inter-communicate with each other using various lines like high-speed buses. This can also be referred to as distributed systems or as loosely coupled systems. The functioning and size of the processors may vary in a distributed operating system. The processors in distributed operating systems are referred to as computers, sites, nodes and so on.

Advantages of the distributed operating systems are given below:

- The users at one side can access and use the resources that are present on a different site using the resource sharing facility of the distributed operating system.

- The data exchange speed between one another is increased using the electronic mail.

- Even if a site in a distributed operating system fails, other sites will be unaffected and they can continue to operate potentially.

- The distributed operating system provides better services to its customers.

- The load on a host computer is reduced.

- The data processing delay is reduced.

Network operating System

The network operating system runs on a server. The network operating system is responsible for providing the server with capabilities like data management, group management, user management, application management, secularity management and a few other networking functions. The network operating system is responsible for the file sharing and printer axis among all the computers that are present in the network. These networks are usually private networks, local area networks or any other networks. The LINUX operating system can be used as a powerful and efficient network operating system.

The advantages and disadvantages of the network operating systems are discussed below:

Advantages of the network operating systems:

- The stability of the centralized servers is high.

- The server can manage the security.

- If there are any updates to the hardware or new technologies, they can be integrated easily into the system.

- With network operating systems, it is possible to remotely access the service from a different type of system from a different location.

Disadvantages of the network operating system:

- The initial cost and the cost of maintenance for running a server are high.

- For most of the operations, the servers are dependent on a central location.

- Frequent updates and regular maintenance are required.

Real Time operating System

The real-time operating system can be defined as a data processing system where the required time interval for process and response to the inputs is so quick that it can control the environment. All the real-time processing is online but it is not necessary for the online system to be a real-time system. The time taken by a system to respond to a given input and to give the output with the updated information is called the response time. When compared to the response time of online processing, the response time in this method is very quick.

There are two different types of real-time operating system.

Hard real-time systems

Real-time systems guarantee the user with completion of critical tasks on time. The secondary storage is missing or is limited in the case of the real-time systems. The data can be stored in ROM format. In real-time systems you cannot find virtual memory.

Soft real-time systems

Unlike the hard real-time systems, the soft real-time systems are less restrictive. A soft real-time system prioritizes critical tasks with high priority and will retain those priorities until the task is completed. When compared to the hard real-time systems, soft real-time systems are allocated with limited utility. For example, advanced scientific projects like planetary Rovers, deep sea exploration, virtual reality, multimedia etc. can use soft real time systems.

Chapter 2:
Components of LINUX

The LINUX operating system is the most popular version of the UNIX OS. Linux was basically designed to be compatible with UNIX. The functionalities of both the operating systems are very similar.

Components of the Linux System

The Linux operating system mainly comprises of three components. They are as follows:

- Kernel - The kernel is considered to be the LINUX operating system's core part and it is the one that is responsible for the operating system's major activities. The kernel directly interacts with the hardware and it has various modules within it. The kernel hides all the low-level hardware details by providing the required abstraction to the application programs or system.

- System Library - System libraries can be considered as the special programs or functions with which the system utilities or the application programs access the features of the kernel. Almost all of the functionality that these libraries can implement an operating system implements as well. For accessing rights, the system libraries won't require the code of kernel module.

- System Utility - System utilities are nothing but programs that are responsible for performing specialized and individual tasks.

Basic Features

Here are some of the important features of the Linux OS.

- Portable - Portability means software can work on different types of hardware in same way. Linux kernel and application programs support their installation on any kind of hardware platform.

- Open Source - Linux source code is freely available and it is community based development project. Multiple teams work in collaboration to enhance the capability of Linux operating system and it is continuously evolving.

- Multi-User - Linux is a multiuser system means multiple users can access system resources like memory/ ram/ application programs at same time.

- Multiprogramming - Linux is a multiprogramming system means multiple applications can run at same time.

- Hierarchical File System - Linux provides a standard file structure in which system files/ user files are arranged.

- Shell - Linux provides a special interpreter program that can be used to execute commands of the operating system. It can be used to do various types of operations, called application programs etc.

- Security - Linux provides user security using authentication features like password protection/ controlled access to specific files/ encryption of data.

Architecture

The following players are part of the Linux system architecture:

- **Hardware layer** - All the peripheral devices like hard disks, CPU, RAM come under the hardware layer.

- **Kernel** - The kernel is the main component or the core component of an operating system. This directly communicates with the system hardware providing the upper layer components with low level services.

- **Shell** – The Shell can be considered as an interface between the user and the kernel. The shell accepts comments given by the users and executes the kernel functions.

- **Utilities** - Utility programs are those that give or provide users with most of the operating system's functionalities.

Chapter 3:
The Linux Kernel

In this chapter, we will learn about the Linux kernel. The Linux kernel is the computer operating system that is similar to UNIX. Worldwide, the Linux kernel is being used widely. The Linux operating system is completely based on Linux kernel and is it deployed on traditional computer systems that are distributed by the LINUX distributions and also on embedded devices like routers. The android mobile operating system which works on mobile and tablet computers is also built using the Linux kernel.

In 1991, Linus Torvalds, a student of computer science from Finland, created the Linux kernel to be used on his PC alone, without actually intending it to be used on other platforms, but gradually developed it such that it could run on different computer architectures. The new operating system gained huge attention from developers, who were interested in adapting code from other projects involving free software, to develop it further. Nearly, 12,000 software developers contributed to the development of the Linux Kernel. Nearly, 1200 companies were involved in its development.

The Linux Kernel is free and was developed by software developers all over the world. It is open source software that means; the source code of the kernel can be accessed and modified by anyone. LKML or the Linux Kernel mailing list is a mailing list that involves the discussions on the development of the Linux Kernel.

The following diagram illustrates the kernel as the interface between the user applications and the CPU, memory and other devices

Programming language

The GNU Compiler Collection (GCC) supports a C language version (developed by incorporating into standard C, several changes and extensions), which has been used to write the Linux kernel. Along with the C language, assembly language has also been used to write several small parts of the code. Since GCC supports several extensions of the C language, it remained the only compiler having the capability to build the Linux kernel for many days.

Finding the Linux Kernel Sources

The Kernel sources can be found in most of the Linux distributions. The Linux Kernel that you install onto your system was developed using these sources. They can be found on ftp://ftp.cs.helsinki.fi and are shadowed by other websites. In case you do not have Internet access, you can get hold of a CD ROM from vendors who charge a very reasonable price for offering snapshots of prominent websites. Some vendors with periodic updates also render subscription services. An alternative and best source available is the local user group of Linux.

Arrangement of the kernel sources

Several directories can be found at the highest level of source tree /usr/src/Linux:

Arch

The kernel code specific to the architecture is present in this subdirectory. It is further divided into subdirectories, one for each architecture. Alpha and i386 are some examples of the subdirectories.

Include

The include files required for building the kernel code are present in this subdirectory. It is also further divided into subdirectories, one for each architecture. Editing the kernel makefile and then rerunning the configuration program of the kernel can change the architecture.

Init

The kernel's initialization code is present in this directory. To understand the working of a kernel, this could be a good place to start.

MM

These can be related to the memory management present in this directory. The code related to the memory management for each architecture is present in arch/*/mm/.

Drivers

This is the place that consists of the device drivers of the system. These device drivers are further classified into different classes

IPC

The code for interprocess communication is present in this directory.

Modules

The modules that are created and held by this directory.

FS

The code of the filesystem is present in this directory. This directory has several subdivisions one for each file system.

Kernel

It consists of the kernel code. The kernel code specific to the architecture can be found in arch/*/kernel.

Net

It consists of the networking code of the kernel.

Lib

The library code of the kernel is present in this directory. The library code specific to an architecture is present in arch/*/lib/.

Scripts

The scripts that are used during the configuration of the kernel are present in this directory.

Chapter 4:
Linux Processes

For Linux to efficiently deal with the processes taking place in the system, a data structure 'task_struct' is used to represent each process in the system. In Linux, the terms process and task can be interchanged. The data structure task_struct has an array of pointers known as the task vector.

The task vector's size limits the number of processes happening in the system. The maximum number of entries is 512 by default. Creation of a new process results in the allocation of a new task_struct from the memory. Adding it into the task vector completes the creation. The current pointer points the current running processes, so that they are easier to find.

In addition to the normal process, Linux also supports real time processes. These real time processes are expected to respond very swiftly to external requests, and hence are termed as real time. So, the scheduler treats these real-time processes a bit differently when compared to the normal processes. The complex data structure task_struct is made simple by dividing it into the following functional areas:

State

The state of a process gets changed after its execution, depending on the circumstances. Each Linux process has one of the following states:

Running

In this state, the process is ready to run or is currently running in the system. Ready to run means the process is ready to be taken up by one of the system processors for execution.

Waiting

The waiting state means the process is waiting for the occurrence of an event or waiting for a resource. In Linux, the waiting processes are differentiated into two types. They are: interruptible waiting processes and uninterruptible waiting processes. Signals can interrupt waiting processes or certain waiting processes. Such waiting processes are termed as interruptible. The waiting processes, which the signals cannot interrupt, are termed as uninterruptible.

Stopped

The process should receive a signal to stop. The process has been stopped, usually by receiving a signal. A process needs to be in the stopped state to be debugged.

Zombie

This is a dead process, yet consists of the data structure task_struct in the task vector. Hence, it is known as a zombie.

Scheduling Information

This is the information which the scheduler uses, to decide the order in which the processes should run.

Identifiers

In a system, a process identifier that is a number identifies every process.

Inter-Process Communication

The important IPC mechanisms supported by Linux are signals, pipes, message queues, shared memory, semaphores etc.; you will learn them in detail in following chapters.

Links

Processes are not independent of one another in system running on Linux. All processes have parent processes. The only process that does not have a parent process is the initial process. The creation of new processes does not take place. What actually takes place is the cloning of processes from the processes that have occurred previously. The task structure that represents a process also points to the parent process and also to the siblings (processes that share the same parent). The pstree command can be used to view the relationships that run between the processes:

init(1)-+-crond(98)

    |-emacs(387)

    |-gpm(146)

    |-inetd(110)

    |-kerneld(18)

    |-kflushd(2)

    |-klogd(87)

    |-kswapd(3)

```
|-login(160)---bash(192)---emacs(225)
|-lpd(121)
|-mingetty(161)
|-mingetty(162)
|-mingetty(163)
|-mingetty(164)
|-login(403)---bash(404)---pstree(594)
|-sendmail(134)
|-syslogd(78)
`-update(166)
```

Times and Timers

Another important duty of the kernel is keeping track of the time taken for creating a process. It also keeps track of the CPU time consumed by the process during its lifespan. As the clock ticks, the kernel keeps on updating the time spent by the current process in the system.

File system

Linux is very flexible when it comes to supporting file systems. It supports a wide variety of file systems, which helps in its coexistence with other popular operating systems. Linux supports a total of 15 file systems. They are:

ext

ext2

vfat

affs

minix

sysv

hpfs

ncp

umsdos

iso9660

ufs

xia

msdos

smb

proc

Many more file systems will be added in future. The processes are free to open or close any file they need.

Virtual memory

Virtual memory is used by most of the processes. It is the duty of the Linux Kernel to track the mapping of virtual memory to the physical memory. Some processes such as Daemons and kernel threads do not use virtual memory.

Processor Specific Context

One can think of a process as an aggregate of the current state of the system. When a process runs, it uses the registers of the processors, stacks etc. and that is the context of the process. After the suspension of the process, it is a must to save the context of the process in task_struct data structure. This is to restore the context of a process after restarting it.

How Linux Organizes Data

For increasing the effectiveness of an operating system, it should organize its data in a good way. The LINUX operating system also organizes its data for making the most out of it. In this chapter, we will learn how the Linux operating system organizes its data. If you have worked with other operating systems like Microsoft Windows, you may find it easy learning how the Linux operating system organizes its data as most of the operating systems organize their data in similar ways.

Devices

LINUX receives, stores and sends its data to and from devices. Every device corresponds to the hardware unit like a serial port keyboard. It is not necessary for a device to have a hardware counterpart. The kernel can create many pseudodevices that act like devices but they do not physically exist. A given hardware unit can have more than one device connected to it, for example, the LINUX operating system will show the partitions of disk drives as a separate devices.

Some of the typical Linux devices are listed in the table given below.

Device	Description
atibm	Bus mouse
audio	Sound card
cdrom	CD-ROM drive

console	Current virtual console
fd n	Floppy drive (n designates the drive; for example, fd0 is the first floppy drive)
ftape	Streaming tape drive not supporting rewind
hd xn	Non-SCSI hard drive (x designates the drive and n designates the partition; for example, hda1 is the first partition of the first non-SCSI hard drive)
inportbm	Bus mouse
lp n	Parallel port (n designates the device number; for example, lp0 is the first parallel port)
modem	Modem
mouse	Mouse
nftape	Streaming tape drive supporting rewind
nrft n	Streaming tape drive supporting rewind (n designates the device number; for example, nrft0 is the first streaming tape drive)
nst n	Streaming SCSI tape drive not supporting rewind

	(*n* designates the device number; for example, nst0 is the first streaming SCSI tape drive)
null	Pseudodevice that accepts unlimited output
printer	Printer
psaux	Auxiliary pointing device, such as a trackball, or the knob on IBM's Thinkpad
rft *n*	Streaming tape drive not supporting rewind (*n* designates the device number; for example, rft0 is the first streaming tape drive)
scd *n*	SCSI device (*n* designates the device number; for example, scd0 is the first SCSI device)
sd *xn*	SCSI hard drive (*x* designates the drive and *n* designates the partition; for example, sda1 is the first partition of the firs SCSI hard drive)
sr *n*	SCSI CD-ROM (*n* designates the drive; for example, sr0 is the first SCSI CD-ROM)
st *n*	Streaming SCSI tape drive supporting rewind (*n* designates the device number; for example, st0 is the first streaming SCSI tape drive)

tty *n*	Virtual console (*n* designates the particular virtual console; for example, tty0 is the first virtual console)
ttyS *n*	Modem (*n* designates the port; for example, ttyS0 is an incoming modem connection on the first serial port)
zero	Pseudo device that supplies an inexhaustible stream of zero-bytes

Chapter 5:
Linux File Systems

Whether you are using the LINUX operating system or the Microsoft Windows operating system, you will have to perform a partition first before you can store any data on it. Whenever you format of partition in Linux, the LINUX operating system will write a special data that is known as the file system on that partition.

Every operating system supports its own set of file systems. Compare to the Windows operating system, the LINUX operating system supports a range of file system types. The file systems that are supported by the LINUX operating system are listed in the table given below.

Filesystem	Description
coherent	A filesystem compatible with that used by Coherent Unix
ext	The predecessor of the ext2 filesystem; supported for compatibility
ext2	The standard Linux filesystem
hpfs	A filesystem compatible with that used by IBM's OS/2

iso9660	The standard filesystem used on CD-ROMs
minix	An old Linux filesystem, still occasionally used on floppy diskettes
msdos	A filesystem compatible with Microsoft's FAT filesystem, used by MS-DOS and Windows
nfs	A filesystem compatible with Sun's Network File System
ntfs	A filesystem compatible with that used by Microsoft Windows NT's NTFS filesystem
sysv	A filesystem compatible with that used by AT&T's System V Unix
vfat	A filesystem compatible with Microsoft's FAT32 filesystem, used by Windows 9x
xenix	A filesystem compatible with that used by Xenix

Chapter 6:
Inter Process Communication

Inter process communication is a process where various communication protocols are used to share data between different processes. Servers and Clients are two different types of applications that use inter-process communication. In this application, the clients are mapped to single or multiple servers to whom they request information in the form of data and the server or servers send in the data. Different platforms provide different ways for the clients to access data. For example, Linux is a platform and below are the mechanisms that it provides for inter-process communication to take place:

1. The Kernel or processes send in signals to the process that they wish to communicate with. They are the cheapest forms of inter-process communication that the Linux platform provides. Signals can be in the form of events or states. These two have the same work - that is that they infer or notify that some change has occurred in the process of one process or kernel.

2. "|" is called a pipe that sets up by the shell that the platform uses to transfer input from one process to another. The two ends of the pipe are linked as a one to one communication mechanism with the help of file descriptors on both ends. These file descriptors are associated with single functionality that is read only or write only. So the end from which the details are to be sent uses the reading file descriptor that reads the data from the process and the end where the data has to be taken from will use the writing descriptor so that it can write the data received. Since the data flow is single sided the mechanism is known as half- duplex mechanism.

Processes that have a parent- child relationship where the parents create the pipes to their children through which they can communicate with them and also create pipes between their children so that they can communicate between themselves can use these pipes. This happens because the file descriptors are copied into their address spaces.

3. First in first out pipes are also known as named pipes are also used in the same way as unnamed pipes are used. The only difference is that these are used when the processes are not related to each other. The processes using these pipes communicate using FIFO files instead of file descriptors. FIFO files also have the same mechanism as file descriptors where one FIFO file has reading functionality and the other has reading functionality. So, we can say that this mechanism is also half- duplex.

4. For single or multiple processes to read or write from single or multiple process we use Message queues. In other words, we can say that this mechanism is similar to that of a post box. The process that wants to share the data comes and places the packet containing the data onto the message queue and leaves. The process that wants to take the data comes and takes the packet. This saves a lot of time, as the process sharing the data needn't wait for the other process. There are 2 different specifications of the message queues 1. SysvV message queues where the messages that are being sent contain a number so that the process receiving the message can take the data matching a particular number or accept everything except the packet that matches a particular number.2. POSIX is a mechanism that works in priority. It sends the packets in their priority order. This priority number is attached with the packets when the process is sending them. So when the other process receives the details the data in the highest priority packet is sent first.

5. There are counters that queue the order of process that will receive the shared resources one after another. These counters are known as semaphores. They lock the shared resource so that only one process can access the shared resource. Once this process is done using the resource, it is released then the process that is next in priority will get the resource or the process that requested the resource irrespective of the priority will get the resource. This is similar to SysV and POSIX mechanisms of the message queues. So they are known as SysV semaphores and POSIX semaphores.

6. The mechanism in which multiple processes share the memory space available is known as the shared memory mechanism. This will help the 2 or more processes that share the memory to communicate more efficiently so that there is less interference of the kernel. Even in shared memory there are 2 types that are SysV shared memory and POSIX shared memory that works in the same way. There the priority is considered in one and it is not considered in another.

Chapter 7:
Linux Shell

As you already know, a computer can only understand 0's and 1's. It is called the binary language. In the first generation of computing, the instructions were given to the computer in the binary language. The binary language is extremely difficult to understand. Reading and writing in the binary language is a time consuming and a difficult task to do. For solving this problem, a special program called the shell was introduced to the operating systems. This special program known as Shell will accept the commands given in English and checks if it is a valid command.

If the given command is valid, it will pass that command to the kernel. The shell can be considered as a user program that makes the interaction between the user and the kernel easy. Shell is a command line interpreter. Shell can take inputs from the file or from a standard input device like a keyboard. Though shell is not part of the kernel, it uses the kernel for creating files, executing programs etc.

In simple words, the shell can be considered as an interface between the user and the system kernel. The shell can execute some of the basic commands even without passing them to the kernel.

If you wish to know the available shells that are present in your system, you can check it using the following command.

$ cat /etc/shells

Though there are many shells available within an operating system, all of them are designed to do the same job. Different shells have different syntaxes and different built in functions. In MS-DOS, the command.com is a shell that the Windows operating system uses. When compared to the shells present in LINUX, it is not a powerful one.

All the shells take the commands from the user through the file or through an input device such as a keyboard and will convey the message to the LINUX operating system saying what the user requires.

If the user gives the command using an input device like a keyboard, it is known as the command line interface. You can know the current shells on which you are working by using the command given below.

$ echo $SHELL

Shell Script

All the shells are interactive. This means that a shell accepts the user, and can excuse them. You can either give your commands one after another or you can store all these commands in a sequence into a text file and can give this to the shell to execute them. Giving the commands all at once is called as shell scripting.

Shell scripting can be defined as:

"Shell Script is series of command written in plain text file. Shell script is just like batch file is MS-DOS but have more power than the MS-DOS batch file."

Why to Write Shell Script?

- The user can give their input directly or through a file to a shell script and it will give the output on the screen.

- You can create your own commands using shell script.

- Shell scripting will save you a lot of time by taking all the commands at once.

- Shell scripting can be used for automating tasks that we use in day-to-day life.

- Using scripting you can also automate the system administration part.

How to write Shell Script?

For writing a script you should follow the given steps:

- You should use an editor such as mcedit or vi for writing shell script.

- After writing this set of commands in the shell script, you should set the execute permissions the script prepared. The syntax for executing the permission is given below:

Syntax: chmod permission your-script-name

Examples:

$ chmod +x your-script-name

$ chmod 755 your-script-name

Using this website read write execute(7) for the system admin or owner. For setting the permission for a group you should only use read and execute(5).

- Now you should execute your written script following the syntax given below

syntax: bash your-script-name

sh your-script-name

./your-script-name

Examples:

$ bash bar

$ sh bar

$ ./bar

You should note that ./ indicates your current working directly and '.' (Dot) indicates the execution of the commander file a given present in the current shell without initializing a new copy of the shell. The syntax for using the '.' (Dot) is given below.

Syntax: . command-name

Example: $. foo

- Now you can write your own shell script using the vi command list or any other editors and create your new shell script called the First Shell.

$ vi first

#

My first shell script

#

clear

echo "First Shell"

After saving the script, you can run your prescription by following the steps given below.

$ ./first

Executing this, it will not run your prescription as we haven't set the permissions to execute the script. For setting the permission you can type the command given below.

$ chmod 755 first

$ ./first

The screen will be cleared at first and then the message given in your shell script will be printed.

Output: First Shell

•Script Command(s)	Meaning
$ vi first	Start vi editor
# # My first shell script #	# followed by any text is considered as comment. Comment gives more information about script, logical explanation about shell script. *Syntax:* # comment-text
clear	clear the screen
echo "First Shell"	To print message or value of variables on screen, we use echo command, general form of echo command is as follows *syntax:* echo "Message"

Basic Command Line Editing

For editing and recalling commands, the key combinations given below can be used.

CTRL + L: Clears the screen.

CTRL + W: Delete the word starting at cursor.

CTRL + U: Clear the line i.e. Delete all words from command line.

Up and Down arrow keys: Recall commands.

Tab: Auto-complete files, directory, command names and much more.

CTRL + R: Search through previously used commands.

CTRL + C: Cancel currently running commands.

CTRL + T: Swap the last two characters before the cursor.

ESC + T: Swap the last two words before the cursor.

CTRL + H: Delete the letter starting at cursor.

Executing a Command

For executing a command, you can just type your comment on the terminal and press the enter key. We will try executing the date command. The date command will give the current date and time as output.

date

Sample outputs:

Wed Jan 27 05:35:56 IST 2015

Bash Shell Commands (source http://ss64.com/bash/)

Here is a list of all the bash commands given in alphabetical order.

alias	Create an alias •
apropos	Search Help manual pages (man -k)
apt-get (Debian/Ubuntu)	Search for and install software packages
aptitude (Debian/Ubuntu)	Search for and install software packages
aspell	Spell Checker
awk sort/validate/index	Find and Replace text, database
basename	Strip directory and suffix from filenames
bash	GNU Bourne-Again SHell
bc	Arbitrary precision calculator language
bg	Send to background
break	Exit from a loop
builtin	Run a shell builtin
bzip2	Compress or decompress named file(s)
cal	Display a calendar
case	Conditionally perform a command
cat content of files	Concatenate and print (display) the
cd	Change Directory

cfdisk	Partition table manipulator for Linux
chgrp	Change group ownership
chmod	Change access permissions
chown	Change file owner and group
chroot directory	Run a command with a different root
chkconfig	System services (runlevel)
cksum	Print CRC checksum and byte counts
clear	Clear terminal screen
cmp	Compare two files
comm	Compare two sorted files line by line
cp	Copy one or more files to another location
cron	Daemon to execute scheduled commands
crontab	Schedule a command to run at a later time
csplit	Split a file into context-determined pieces
cut	Divide a file into several parts
date	Display or change the date & time
dc	Desk Calculator
dd headers, boot records	Convert and copy a file, write disk
	ddrescue Data recovery tool
declare •	Declare variables and give them attributes
df	Display free disk space
diff	Display the differences between two files
diff3	Show differences among three files

dig	DNS lookup
dir	Briefly list directory contents
dircolors	Color setup for `ls'
dirname	Convert a full pathname to just a path
dirs	Display list of remembered directories
dmesg	Print kernel & driver messages
du	Estimate file space usage
echo	Display message on screen •
egrep	Search file(s) for lines that match an extended expression
eject	Eject removable media
enable	Enable and disable builtin shell commands •
env	Environment variables
ethtool	Ethernet card settings
eval	Evaluate several commands/arguments
exec	Execute a command
exit	Exit the shell
expect	Automate arbitrary applications accessed over a terminal
expand	Convert tabs to spaces
export	Set an environment variable
expr	Evaluate expressions
false	Do nothing, unsuccessfully
fdformat	Low-level format a floppy disk
fdisk	Partition table manipulator for Linux

fg	Send job to foreground
fgrep	Search file(s) for lines that match a fixed string
file	Determine file type
find	Search for files that meet a desired criteria
fmt	Reformat paragraph text
fold	Wrap text to fit a specified width.
for	Expand words, and execute commands
format	Format disks or tapes
free	Display memory usage
fsck	File system consistency check and repair
ftp	File Transfer Protocol
function	Define Function Macros
fuser file	Identify/kill the process that is accessing a
gawk	Find and Replace text within file(s)
getopts	Parse positional parameters
grep pattern	Search file(s) for lines that match a given
groupadd	Add a user security group
groupdel	Delete a group
groupmod	Modify a group
groups	Print group names a user is in
gzip	Compress or decompress named file(s)
hash argument	Remember the full pathname of a name

head	Output the first part of file(s)
help	Display help for a built-in command •
history	Command History
hostname	Print or set system name
htop	Interactive process viewer
iconv	Convert the character set of a file
id	Print user and group id's
if	Conditionally perform a command
ifconfig	Configure a network interface
ifdown	Stop a network interface
ifup	Start a network interface up
import image to file	Capture an X server screen and save the
install	Copy files and set attributes
ip	Routing, devices and tunnels
jobs	List active jobs
join	Join lines on a common field
kill	Kill a process by specifying its PID
killall	Kill processes by name
less	Display output one screen at a time
let	Perform arithmetic on shell variables •
link	Create a link to a file
ln	Create a symbolic link to a file
local	Create variables •
locate	Find files

logname	Print current login name
logout	Exit a login shell •
look	Display lines beginning with a given string
lpc	Line printer control program
lpr	Off line print
lprint	Print a file
lprintd	Abort a print job
lprintq	List the print queue
lprm	Remove jobs from the print queue
ls	List information about file(s)
lsof	List open files
make	Recompile a group of programs
man	Help manual
mkdir	Create new folder(s)
mkfifo	Make FIFOs (named pipes)
mkisofs filesystem	Create an hybrid ISO9660/JOLIET/HFS
mknod	Make block or character special files
more	Display output one screen at a time
most	Browse or page through a text file
mount	Mount a file system
mtools	Manipulate MS-DOS files
mtr	Network diagnostics (traceroute/ping)
mv	Move or rename files or directories
mmv	Mass Move and rename (files)

netstat	Networking information
nice	Set the priority of a command or job
nl	Number lines and write files
nohup	Run a command immune to hangups
notify-send	Send desktop notifications
nslookup	Query Internet name servers interactively
open	Open a file in its default application
op	Operator access
passwd	Modify a user password
paste	Merge lines of files
pathchk	Check file name portability
ping	Test a network connection
pkill	Kill processes by a full or partial name.
popd directory	Restore the previous value of the current
pr	Prepare files for printing
printcap	Printer capability database
printenv	Print environment variables
printf	Format and print data •
ps	Process status
pushd directory	Save and then change the current
pv pipe	Monitor the progress of data through a
pwd	Print Working Directory
quota	Display disk usage and limits

quotacheck	Scan a filesystem for disk usage
quotactl	Set disk quotas
ram	ram disk device
rar	Archive files with compression
rcp	Copy files between two machines
read	Read a line from standard input •
readarray	Read from stdin into an array variable •
readonly	Mark variables/functions as readonly
reboot	Reboot the system
rename	Rename files
renice	Alter priority of running processes
remsync	Synchronize remote files via email
return	Exit a shell function
rev	Reverse lines of a file
rm	Remove files
rmdir	Remove folder(s)
rsync	Remote file copy (Synchronize file trees)
screen ssh	Multiplex terminal, run remote shells via
scp	Secure copy (remote file copy)
sdiff	Merge two files interactively
sed	Stream Editor
select	Accept keyboard input
seq	Print numeric sequences
set	Manipulate shell variables and functions

sftp	Secure File Transfer Program
shift	Shift positional parameters
shopt	Shell Options
shutdown	Shutdown or restart linux
sleep	Delay for a specified time
slocate	Find files
sort	Sort text files
source	Run commands from a file '.'
split	Split a file into fixed-size pieces
ssh program)	Secure Shell client (remote login
stat	Display file or filesystem status
strace	Trace system calls and signals
su	Substitute user identity
sudo	Execute a command as another user
sum	Print a checksum for a file
suspend	Suspend execution of this shell •
sync	Synchronize data on disk with memory
tail	Output the last part of file
tar	Store, list or extract files in an archive
tee	Redirect output to multiple files
test	Evaluate a conditional expression
time	Measure Program running time
timeout	Run a command with a time limit
times	User and system times

touch	Change file timestamps
top	List processes running on the system
tput color, position	Set terminal-dependent capabilities,
traceroute	Traceroute to Host
trap set(bourne)	Run a command when a signal is
tr characters	Translate, squeeze, and/or delete
true	Do nothing, successfully
tsort	Topological sort
tty	Print filename of terminal on stdin
type	Describe a command •
ulimit	Limit user resources •
umask	Users file creation mask
umount	Unmounts a device
unalias	Remove an alias •
uname	Print system information
unexpand	Convert spaces to tabs
uniq	Uniquely files
units	Convert units from one scale to another
unrar	Extract files from a rar archive
unset	Remove variable or function names
unshar	Unpack shell archive scripts
until	Execute commands (until error)
uptime	Show uptime

useradd	Create new user account
userdel	Delete a user account
usermod	Modify user account
users	List users currently logged in
uuencode	Encode a binary file
uudecode	Decode a file created by uuencode
v	Verbosely list directory contents (`ls -l -b')
vdir	Verbosely list directory contents (`ls -l -b')
vi	Text Editor
vmstat	Report virtual memory statistics
wait	Wait for a process to complete •
watch	Execute/display a program periodically
wc	Print byte, word, and line counts
whereis	Search the user's $path, man pages and source files for a program
which	Search the user's $path for a program file
while	Execute commands
who	Print all usernames currently logged in
whoami	Print the current user id and name (`id -un')
wget	Retrieve web pages or files via HTTP, HTTPS or FTP
write	Send a message to another user
xargs	Execute utility, passing constructed argument list(s)

xdg-open	Open a file or URL in the user's preferred application.
yes	Print a string until interrupted
zip	Package and compress (archive) files.
.	Run a command script in the current shell
!!	Run the last command again
###	Comment / Remark

The commands that have the '•' are the default shell commands.

Chapter 8:
Command Line Tutorial

ow you know all about Linux and what it consists of, it's time to look at actually using it. I'm going to start with a basic command line tutorial but first you need to know how to open the terminal. This is easy but all systems are different. Use this as a guideline only:

- Mac users should open **Applications, Utilities** and then click on **Terminal.** A shortcut would be to press on **Command+Space**, which will open Spotlight up, after which you can type in the word Terminal. Click on the result when it shows up.

- Linux users should look in **Applications>System** or **Applications>Utilities.** A shortcut is to right click on your desktop and look for the option to "Open in Terminal". If it is there, click on it.

- Windows users can simply type in the word **command** in the search bar on their start menu. Click on the option for **Command Prompt** and it will take you straight to it.

As you know, the command line is where you type your commands and receive an output, or feedback as text. The command line start with a prompt and the text you type is displayed after this prompt. Most of your work will be command work and an example of that is this:

1. ls -l /home/Simon

2. total 3

3. drwxr-xr-x 2 Simon users 4096 Mar 23 13:34 bin

4. drwxr-xr-x 18 Simon users 4096 Feb 17 09:12 Documents

5. drwxr-xr-x 2 Simon users 4096 May 05 17:25 public_html

Let's break that code down and see what it all means:

Line 1 always stars with the prompt with your username@bash. We also put a command in there – ls –and the command is always the first thing that you type. Following that are what we all command line arguments. Be aware that there must always be a space between the command and the first argument. The very first command line argument is (-l) and this is called an option. These are used to change the way the command behaves, they are always listed before any other argument and start with (-) a dash.

Lines 2 to 5 - These are outputs that come from running the command that you typed in. nearly all commands will produce an output and it will always be listed immediately under the command issue. Other commands will just do as they are told to and will not produce any information unless it results in an error.

Line 6 – Again, we get the prompt. Once the command has been run, the terminal is ready for use again and will display the prompt. If there is no prompt showing, the command is most likely still running.

Shortcuts

While the terminal may seem a little overwhelming to a new user, there is nothing to be worried about, Linux is packed full of handy shortcuts that will make your life so much easier. I will go through some of them as I go through this chapter so make a note of them as you come across them – they won't just make life easy, they can also stop you from making mistakes like typographical errors.

Your first shortcut is this – whenever you enter in a command, it is stored in a history and you can work your way through this history by using the arrow keys – the up and down ones. So, you don't need to type out commands that you have already typed; if you need to enter the same one again, simply use the arrow keys to find it. If you want to edit the commands, use the left and right arrow keys to put the cursor where you need it to make the change.

Basic Navigation

The very first command I want you to look at is **pwd -** this stands for Print Working Directory. Many of the Linux commands are shortened to abbreviations and his makes it much easier to remember them. So, this command does exactly what it says it does – prints the working directory to the screen. Give it a go:

- pwd

- /home/Simon

Many of the commands that you type in on the terminal need you to be in the right location to work. As you will be moving around quite a bit, it will be easy to lose yourself. Simply typing **pwd** in at the command prompt will tell you your location so make use of it to keep in touch with your location.

The next thing you might want to know is what exactly in in the location you are in. The command to find that out is **ls** – short for **list.**

- ls

- bin Documents public_html

Where pwd runs without arguments, ls has a bit more power. In this example, we haven't given it any arguments, so that we will get just a list of what is in the current location. You can do so much more with it, for example:

- ls [options] [location]

The [] square brackets indicate that the text inside them is optional so the command can run with them or without them. The example below show the ls command run in a number of different ways just to give you an idea of what it can do:

1. ls

2. bin Documents public_html

3. ls -l

4. total 3

5. drwxr-xr-x 2 Simon users 4096 Mar 23 13:34 bin

6. drwxr-xr-x 18 Simon users 4096 Feb 17 09:12 Documents

7. drwxr-xr-x   2 Simon   users   4096   May   05   17:25 public_html

8. ls /etc

9. a2ps.cfg aliases alsa.d cups fonts my.conf systemd

10. ...

11. ls -l /etc

12. total 3

13. -rwxr-xr-x 2 root root 123 Mar 23 13:34 a2ps.cfg

14. -rwxr-xr-x 18 root root 78 Feb 17 09:12 aliases

15. drwxr-xr-x 2 Simon users 4096 May 05 17:25 alsa.d

16. ...

Let us look at that in more detail:

Line 1 - ls in its absolute most basic format – the result is a list of the contents of the directory we are in

Line 4 - ls with one command line option – (-l). This indicates that we want to do a long listing, which consists of:

- The first character indicates the file type – normal (-) or directory (d)

- The following 9 characters are file or directory permissions

- The next file is the number of the blocks

- The next field indicates the file or directory owner

- The next field indicates the group that the directory or file belongs to

- Next is the size of the file

- Next is the file modification time

- Finally is the name of the directory or file

Line 10 - ls is run with a command line argument this time, (/etc.) – which is telling ls that it shouldn't list the current directory, instead I should list the contents of the directory

Line 13 - ls is run with a command line argument and a command line argument this time, resulting in the directory /etc. being listed as a long

Lines 12 and 18 – these indicate that some of the commands have been cut out, just for the sake of this tutorial; if you actually run those commands, you will get a much longer listing of directories and files.

Paths

In these last commands, we started to introduce the path. It is important that you learn what these are and how to use them as you cannot be proficient in the Linux language until you are. When we talk about a directory or a file on the command line, we are talking about a path. As it is in your hometown, or neighborhood, a path is a way of getting somewhere, in this case to a specific directory or file on the system.

Absolute and Relative Paths

We use two different paths – absolute and relative – to refer to a directory or file. Either can be used, as they will both take you to the same place on the system. To start with, you need to understand hat Linux is known as a hierarchical structure. Right at the top is the **root directory,** indicated by (/) a single backslash. The root directory contains sub-directories, and these have their own sub-directories, and so on. Any of these sub-directories can contain files.

An absolute path is to specify a particular file or directory that is relative to the root directory they are identifiable by the a/ that they all begin with. The relative path specifies a file or directory relative to your current location in the system. They do not start with the / backslash.

Have a look at this example:

- pwd

- /home/Simon

- ls Documents

- file1.txt file2.txt file3.txt

- ...

- ls /home/Simon/Documents

- file1.txt file2.txt file3.txt

- ...

Line 1 – pwd is run to confirm your current location

Line 4 - ls is run with a relative path. Documents is the name of a directory that is the current location but, depending on where you are in the system, this command can provide different results. If you were on the home directory of another system user, that command would simply provide you with a list of the contents of their own Documents directory.

Line 7 – ls is run with an absolute path. This command is not reliant on where you are in the system; the result will be exactly the same wherever you are.

As you learn Linux, it will soon become apparent that there are loads of different ways to get things done. The following are called building blocks and they will help you to build up your paths:

- **~ (tilde)** – a shortcut for the home directory. For example, if your home directory were called /home/Simon, you could refer to the Documents directory with a path that goes something like /home/Simon/Documents or you could just type ~/Documents

- **. (dot)** – A reference to the current directory. Take the example we did earlier where line 4 referred to Documents with a relative path. We could also have written it as ./documents

- **.. (dotdot)** – A reference to the parent directory. This can be used any number of times in a single path if you want to keep on traversing upwards through the hierarchy. For example, if you were in /home/Simon, you could simply type in **ls../../** and you would get a listing of the root directory as your output.

Now you can start to see that you can refer to locations in a number of ways. As to which way you should use, the answer is you can use any of them. If you make a reference to a directory or file on the command line, you are referring to a path and that can be made up with any of the elements we talked about. The best way is whichever way you find the easiest.

Have a look at these examples:

- pwd
- /home/Simon
- ls ~/Documents
- file1.txt file2.txt file3.txt
- …
- ls ./Documents
- file1.txt file2.txt file3.txt
- …
- ls /home/Simon/Documents
- file1.txt file2.txt file3.txt
- …
- ls ../../
- bin boot dev etc home lib var
- …
- ls /
- bin boot dev etc home lib var
- …

Have a go at inputting these into the command line on your system – I promise that they will begin to make a bit more sense to you. Make sue you take the time out to learn all about paths and understand them as you will use them a lot.

Chapter 9:
Moving Around Linux

When you move around in Linux you can use a command called **cd**. This stands for **change directory** and it works like this;

- cd [location]

If you run cd without using an argument, it will take you to your home directory automatically. You can also run this command without using a location but, usually it is run with one single argument on the command line, and that is the location of the new directory that you want to change to. This is specified as a path and can be a relative or an absolute path using any of the bocks that we talked about in the last chapter,

Have a look at these examples:

- pwd
- /home/Simon
- cd Documents
- ls
- file1.txt file2.txt file3.txt
- ...
- cd /
- pwd
- /
- ls

- bin boot dev etc home lib var

- ...

- cd ~/Documents

- pwd

- /home/Simon/Documents

- cd ../../

- pwd

- /home

- cd

- pwd

- /home/Simon

Tab Completion

It can become something of a tedious job to keep typing out these paths and you will end up making errors. However, there is a neat mechanism in the command line that can help with this and it's called **tab completion.** When you begin to type out a path, no matter where you are on the command line and what command you are using, you can press the Tab key on your keyboard. This invokes Auto-Complete – if nothing changes, it means that there are a number of possibilities to completing the path. Pressing the Tab button again will show those possibilities. Continue typing your path and then hot Tab again to narrow the possibilities down to the right one. Have a go on your own command line and see how you get on.

Files

The very first thing you have to learn in Linux is that everything is a file. Directories, text files, even your keyboard (but only one that your system can read from), all of them are files. The monitor that your system writes to is a file as well. This isn't going to have any effect on what you do but you do need to keep it in mind. This will help you to understand how Linux works.

Extensionless System

This might take some getting used to but as you work your way through the programming, it will start to make sense. File extensions are usually a set of characters, between two and four, after a dot at the end of the file name. The extension tells you what the file type is. The following is a list of the most common extensions:

- file.exe – a file or program that is executable

- file.txt - a file that is plain text

- file.png – an image file

- file.gif – an image file

- file.jpg - an image file

In systems like Windows, the file extension is very important because the system uses it to see what file type it is dealing with. Linux is different in that it ignores the file system, instead looking into the file itself to see what it is. As an example, you could take a .jpg file that you have on your system, perhaps a photo of your house, and rename it as .txt text file. Linux would ignore that, look in that file and then treat it as the image file it actually is. Sometimes though, it isn't always easy to determine what file type a file should be deemed as and that's where a little command named **file** comes in.

- file [path]

Now, you might be thinking at this point, why has a command line been specified as a path instead of a file? Remember, when a file or a directory is specified on the command line, it is actually a path. Also, directories are nothing more than a specific type of file; a path is used to get us to a particular place in the system and that place is a file.

Linux is Case Sensitive

This is something that you must keep in mind as it is very important, and is one of the biggest causes of all the problems experienced by newcomers to Linux. Many of the other systems are not sensitive to case but Linux is, especially when you are referring to files. It is perfectly possible to have two files or directories with the same names n Linux; they would just contain different case letters.

For example:

- ls Documents
- FILE1.txt File1.txt file1.TXT
- ...
- file Documents/file1.txt
- Documents/file1.txt: ERROR: cannot open 'file1.txt' (No such file or directory)

Linux sees all of these as different files. You should also be aware of case when you are dealing with command line options. Fore example, with the ls command, there are two options – S and s – both of these do something different. One of the most common mistakes is to see options entered in uppercase where they should be lowercase and then wonder why the output isn't what you expected it to be.

Spaces in Names

There is nothing wrong with having spaces in directory and file names but you should be careful with them. A space on the command line is used to separate things – they are how we determine the program name and are able to identify the arguments on the command line. Let's say that you wanted to move to a directory names Holiday Photos. This example would not work:

- ls Documents
- FILE1.txt File1.txt file1.TXT Holiday Photos
- ...
- cd Holiday Photos
- bash: cd: Holiday: No such file or directory

In this example, Holiday Photos is treated as two separate command line arguments. The command cd moves to the directory that is specified on the first argument only so, to get round this and make it work, we need to let the terminal know that Holiday Photos is to be seen as a single command line argument. There are two ways we can do this and both are valid ways.

Quotes

The first way is to enclose Holiday Photos in quite marks – single or double, it doesn't matter which, so long as you use a matching pair. Anything that is written inside the quotes is treated as one single item:

- cd 'Holiday Photos'

- pwd

- /home/Simon/Documents/Holiday Photos

Escape Characters

Another way is to use something called an escape character. This is a backslash (\ ) and what this does is nullify the special meaning that the next character has:

- cd Holiday\ Photos

- pwd

- /home/Simon/Documents/Holiday Photos

In this example, the space that is between the words Holiday and Photo would usually have a special meaning – to separate them as their own individual command line argument. However, because the backslash was put in front, that nullified that meaning. If you use the tab completion that I talked about earlier, before you come across a space inserted in the directory name, the terminal will escape the spaces automatically for you.

Hidden Files and Directories

Linux has a very nice mechanism for telling you that a directory or file has been hidden. If the name of the file or directory starts with a full stop (.) it is classed as hidden. There are no special commands or actions needed to hide a file or directory. There are a number of reasons why you might want to hide a file or a directory. For example, you might have another user who hides their configuration fees so they don't get in your way.

To hide a file or directory, simply add a full stop to the start of the name or, if you have already created the file, simply rename it with that full stop in the front. In the same way, you can remove the full stop from a file or directory to unhide it just be renaming it.

One thing to keep in mind – the ls command will NOT list any directories or files that are hidden unless you modify the command by adding in the command line option –a. Only then will it list anything that has been hidden.

- ls Documents
- FILE1.txt File1.txt file1.TXT
- ...
- ls -a Documents
- . .. FILE1.txt File1.txt file1.TXT .hidden .file.txt
- ...

Manual Pages

These are available as a set of pages that tells you what every single command means – what they do, how they work, how to run them and the command line arguments that each one will accept. Some of them will be a little difficult to understand for a newcomer to Linux but they are consistent. Once you get the hang of each one, they will start to mean something to you and you will find them easier to work with. Manual pages are invoked with this command:

- man <command to look up>

Example:

- man ls
- Name
- ls - list directory contents
- Synopsis
- ls [option] ... [file] ...

Searching

You can search through the Manual Pages for a specific keyword. This is helpful if you need a reminder of what command you need – you know what you want to do but you are not certain of the command that you need to use. In order for this to work though, you might need to have a few attempts at it. You may find that the articular keyword you are searching for shows up in a number of pages and it may take you time to find the right one.

- man -k <search term>

You can also search inside of a manual page. While you are on a page and you want to search for something on that page, press the forward slash (/) button and follow it up with the search term. Press enter and your results will appear. If there are numerous instances of the search term, you can press 'n' to move through them.

More on Running Commands

Much of being good at Linux is about knowing the right command line options to use to modify the way the commands behave to suit your requirements. Most commands have both a long and a shorthand version. For example, above we talked about hidden files – we can use the command –a or we can use –all to list all directory entries and any hidden files. The first is the shorthand version while the second is the longhand; merely more readable to the human eye. You can use either version; it makes no difference because they both do the same thing. There is an advantage to using longhand and that is that you may find it easier to remember what function your commands are doing. However, an advantage of the shorthand method is that you can chain a number of commands together:

- pwd
- /home/Simon
- ls -a
- ls --all
- ls -alh

Command line options written in longhand start with a pair of dashes (--) while the shorthand version starts with one single dash (-). The single dash can be used to invoke a number of options by putting all the letters that indicate these options together following the dash.

Making a Directory

As I mentioned before, Linux is a hierarchical system and, as time goes by, you will find that you have built up quite a lot of data. Because of this, you should create a system of directories so that you data can be organized in a much more manageable way. Get into the habit of creating directories for new stuff and storing the old under their correct directory.

Creating a directory is easy; we simply use the command **mkdir**, shorthand for Make Directory.

- mkdir [options] <Directory>

You can use mkdir and only supply a directory name and it will make one for you:

- pwd
- /home/Simon
- ls
- bin Documents public_html
- mkdir linuxtutorialwork
- ls
- bin Documents linuxtutorialwork public_html

Let's look at that a little closer:

Line 1 – We start off by checking our current location

Line 2 – We then run a listing so that we know exactly what that directory contains

Line 7 – We run the mkdir command and make a directory named linuxtutorialwork. – Remember, when we give the directory name in the command line, we are giving a path.

The following are a few more examples on ways to create directories:

- mkdir /home/Simon/foo
- mkdir ./blah
- mkdir ../dir1
- mkdir ~/linuxtutorialwork/dir2

There are some very useful options for mkdir. The first of those is –p, which is telling the command mkdir that it should create parent directories as and when needed. The second is –v, which commands mkdir to tell us what it's doing.

The first example is with the –p option:

- mkdir -p linuxtutorialwork/foo/bar
- cd linuxtutorialwork/foo/bar
- pwd
- /home/Simon/linuxtutorialwork/foo/bar

The second is the same example but using the –v option instead.

- mkdir -pv linuxtutorialwork/foo/bar
- mkdir: created directory 'linuxtutorialwork/foo'

- mkdir: created directory 'linuxtutorialwork/foo/bar'
- cd linuxtutorialwork/foo/bar
- pwd
- /home/Simon/linuxtutorialwork/foo/bar

Removing a Directory

It's easy to make a new directory and it is also very easy to delete one. Do keep in mind that, when you delete something on Linux using the command line, there is no option to undo what you did, so be careful, get into the habit of double-checking everything before you go ahead, and delete. The command we use to delete a directory is **rmdir,** short for Remove Directory

- rmdir [options] <Directory>

There are two things to bear in mind here – first, rmdir supports both the -p and the –v options and second, the directory has got to be empty before you can delete it.

- rmdir linuxtutorialwork/foo/bar
- ls linuxtutorialwork/foo

Creating a Blank File

Many commands that are involved with the manipulation of data have a little feature in that, if we refer to a directory that does not yet exist, they will create it for us. We can use this to create blank files with a command named **touch:**

- touch [options] <filename>
- EXAMPLE

- pwd

- /home/Simon/linuxtutorialwork

- ls

- foo

- touch example1

- ls

- example1 foo

The command **touch** is used to modify the modification and access times on files. It isn't always needed but it can be helpful to use if you are testing out a system that relies on file modification or file access times. What is important, as I said earlier, is that if you touch on a file or directory that does not exist, it will be created for you.

Much of what we do in Linux cannot be done automatically but, when you know how a certain command behaves and some of the deeper aspects of the system, you can use the commands in creative ways to get the outcome you desire.

Copying a File or Directory

Sometimes, for whatever reason, you might want to make a copy of a directory or a file. It could be that you are about to make changes to one and you want to make a copy of it so that, if things do go wrong, all is not lost! The command for this is **cp**, which is short for **copy.**

- cp [options] <source> <destination>

There are a number of options for this command, one of which I will demonstrate now:

- ls

- example1 foo

- cp example1 barney

- ls

- barney example1 foo

Did you see that both the destination and the source are paths? These can be referred to using both relative and absolute paths, as per these examples:

- cp /home/Simon/linuxtutorialwork/example2 example3

- cp example2 ../../backups

- cp example2 ../../backups/example4

- cp /home/Simon/linuxtutorialwork/example2 /otherdir/foo/example5

When you use the cp command, it can be either a path to a file or a path to a directory. If it goes to a file, a copy of the source will be created and it will be named by the filename that is specified in the destination path. If the path goes to a directory, the file will be copied into that directory and be named the same as the source.

By default, cp only copied a file. If we use the option –r, which stands for Recursive, we ca copy directories. Recursive means that you want to see a directory and you want to see all of the files and the directories contained in it. For the subdirectories, simply go into them and repeat the command, and so on.

- ls
- barney example1 foo
- cp foo foo2
- cp: omitting directory 'foo'
- cp -r foo foo2
- ls
- barney example1 foo foo2

In this example, the files and the directories that are contained in the directory named foo are copied to foo2.

Moving a File or Directory

If you want to move a directory or a file, you can do so with the command **mv,** which stands for **Move.** It works in pretty much the same way as cp with one small advantage – we don't need to use the –r option to move a directory:

- mv [options] <source> <destination>

Example

- ls
- barney example1 foo foo2
- mkdir backups
- mv foo2 backups/foo3
- mv barney backups/
- ls
- backups example1 foo

Let's break that down:

Line 3 - a new directory called backups has been created

Line 4 - the directory called foo2 was moved into the new backups directory and renamed foo3

Line 7 – The file called barney is moved to the directory called backups. It retained the same name because we didn't give a new destination name

Renaming Files and Directories

Like the **touch** command, we can use the base behavior of the **mv** command in a slightly different way, so that we get a different outcome. As you can see from line 4 in the example above, we might need to give a new name for the directory or the file and, when it is moved, it is renamed. If you specify that the destination is the same directory name as the source, but provide a different name, you have used the **mv** command o change the name of a file or directory

- ls
- backups example1 foo
- mv foo foo3
- ls
- backups example1 foo3
- cd ..
- mkdir linuxtutorialwork/testdir
- mv linuxtutorialwork/testdir /home/Simon/linuxtutorialwork/fred

- ls

- backups example1 foo3 fred

Let's break that down:

Line 3 – the file called foo has been renamed to foo3, using relative paths

Line 6 – we go to the parent directory so that, in the next line, we can show that commands can be run on directories or files even if we are not in their current directory

Line 8 – the directory called testdir was renamed to fred, using a relative path for the source and an absolute path for the destination

Removing a File

The same as it is with **rmdir,** when we remove a file, the action cannot be undone – be very careful what you are doing! We use the command **rm**, short for Remove, to delete or remove a file

- rm [options] <file>

- EXAMPLE

- ls

- backups example1 foo3 fred

- rm example1

- ls

- backups foo3 fred

Removing non empty Directories

The command rm has a number of options that will change the way it works. One very useful one is −r, meaning Recursive, the same as in the command cp. Then we run rm with that −r option, you can remove directories that still contain files and directories

- ls
- backups foo3 fred
- rmdir backups
- rmdir: failed to remove 'backups': Directory not empty
- rm backups
- rm: cannot remove 'backups': Is a directory
- rm -r backups
- ls
- foo3 fred

One good option is to use with r is i, which means interactive. If you use this, whenever you give the command to remove a directory or file, you will get a prompt before each one is removed – this gives you the option of cancelling if you have done this in error.

Wildcards

Wildcards are building blocks that let you come up a pattern that defines a set of directories or files on Linux. If you remember, when we refer to directories and files on the command line, it is a path that we are referring to. When we do this, we can use wildcards within the path, which allows us to turn it into a set of directories or files.

The basic wildcards are:

- - represents zero or more characters
- ? - represents a single character
- [] - represents a range of characters

For the first example, we will look at another one - *. In the example below, we are going to ask to see a list of all entries that begins with the letter "b":

- pwd
- /home/Simon/linuxtutorialwork
- ls
- barry.txt blah.txt bob example.png firstfile foo1 foo2
- foo3 frog.png secondfile thirdfile video.mpeg
- ls b*
- barry.txt blah.txt bob

Under the Hood

This is quite interesting. At first look, you could assume that the ls command is receiving argument b* and is the translating that to bring up the requested matches. However, the translation is being done by bash, which is the program that is responsible for giving us the command line interface. When we put in this command, it will spot that we have included wildcards and, before it can run the command, it will replace that pattern with every single directory or file that matches it. We give this command:

- ls b*

And it is translated into:

- ls barry.txt blah.txt bob

Before the program is executed. The program itself will not see the wildcards and will not know that they have been used. This means that they can be used whenever you want on the command line.

Some More Examples

Let's look at a few more examples of how wildcards behave. For all these following examples, I want you assume that we are working from the directory called linuxtutorialwork and that all of the files listed in the above example are contained in it. While I am using the ls command, please note that wildcards can be used with any command.

In this example, I am going to ask for all the files that end with the .txt extension. I have used an absolute path and it is worth noting that the wildcards work on both absolute and relative paths:

- ls /home/Simon/linuxtutorialwork/*.txt
- barry.txt blah.txt

Now, let's add the ? Operator into the mix. For the next example, I want to look for all files whose second letter is an "i". Note that we are building this pater with the use of more than one wildcard:

- ls ?i*

- firstfile video.mpeg

Or, perhaps we should look for all the files that have a three-letter extension:

- ls *.???

- barry.txt blah.txt example.png frog.png

Lastly, we look at the range operator, denoted by a pair of square brackets []. Unlike the last two wildcards we looked at, both of which specified any character, this range operator will limit you to a specific subset. For example, lets look for all files that begin with an "s" or a "v":

- ls [sv]*
- secondfile video.mpeg

When we use ranges, we can also use a hyphen to include a set. In this example, we want to find all of the files that have a digit in their name:

- ls *[0-9]*
- foo1 foo2 foo3

And we can use the caret (^) to reverse a range. This means that it will look for files with characters that are NOT one of these:

- ls [^a-k]*
- secondfile thirdfile video.mpeg

Some Real World Examples

While these examples show you how the wildcards actually work, you might be asking yourself what they are. Wildcards are used everywhere and, as you go through your learning, you will find tons of ways to use them to make your life much easier. The following are a few examples of how they can be used. This is just a small slice of what they can do – remember that a wildcard can be used whenever a path is specified on the command line. With a bit of clever thinking, you can use them for all sorts of things.

In this example, we are trying to see all of the file types of all of the files in a specific directory:

- file /home/Simon/*

- bin: directory

- Documents: directory

- frog.png: PNG image data

- public_html: directory

- Move all files of type either jpg or png (image files) into another directory.

- mv public_html/*.??g public_html/images/

In the next example, we want to find out what the size and the modification time are of the bash_history file – this resides in the home directory of every user and holds the history of every command that a user has ever input on the command line. You can also use this to locate hidden files:

- ls -lh /home/*/.bash_history

- -rw------- 1 harry users 2.7K Jan 4 07:32 /home/harry/.bash_history

- -rw------- 1 Simon users 3.1K Jun 12 21:16 /home/Simon/.bash_history

Permissions

There are three things that are dictated by a Linux permission – how you read a file, write to a file and execute a file. Each one is denoted with a single letter:

- r read - you may view the contents of the file.

- w write - you may change the contents of the file.

- x execute - you may execute or run the file if it is a program or script.

For each file, we can define three different sets of people whom we can specify permissions for:

- owner - a single person who owns the file. (typically the person who created the file but ownership may be granted to someone else by certain users)

- group - every file belongs to a single group.

- others - everyone else who is not in the group or the owner.

So, that's three permissions and three different sets of people. Really, that s all there is to know about permissions so let's have a look at how we can view them and change them.

View Permissions

Viewing permissions for a particular file involves using the long listing option with the ls command:

- ls -l [path]

Example

- ls -l /home/Simon/linuxtutorialwork/frog.png

- -rwxr----x1harryusers2.7KJan   4
  07:32/home/Simon/linuxtutorialwork/frog.png

In this example, we are looking for the first 10 characters of the output to identify the permissions:

- Character 1 identifies the type of file. A dash (-) indicates a normal file, while a "d" indicates a directory

- Characters 2, 3 and 4 identify the specific permissions for the owner. Letters indicate the permission and a dash (-) indicates that there are no permissions. The example shows that the owner has all three of the permissions.

- The last three characters indicate permission for others. In the example, we can see that they have permission to execute files only, they cannot read or write to them

Change Permissions

To change a permission on a directory or file, we use the **chmod** command, which stands for   **change file mode bits.** The bits are the indicators for the permissions:

- chmod [permissions] [path]

- chmod has permission arguments that are made up of 3 components

The three components are:

- Whom are the permissions being changed for? – UGOA = user, group, others, all

- Are we giving permission or removing it? – indicated with a + or a –

- Which permission is being set? – read , write, execute

Look at the following example to see if it is any clearer to you. We are granting permission for execute to the group and taking permission for write away from the user, or owner

- ls -l frog.png
- -rwxr----x 1 harry users 2.7K Jan 4 07:32 frog.png
- chmod g+x frog.png
- ls -l frog.png
- -rwxr-x--x 1 harry users 2.7K Jan 4 07:32 frog.png
- chmod u-w frog.png
- ls -l frog.png
- -r-xr-x--x 1 harry users 2.7K Jan 4 07:32 frog.png

If you do not want to give individual permissions, you can give multiple permissions at the same time:

- ls -l frog.png
- -rwxr----x 1 harry users 2.7K Jan 4 07:32 frog.png

- chmod g+wx frog.png

- ls -l frog.png

- -rwxrwx--x 1 harry users 2.7K Jan 4 07:32 frog.png

- chmod go-x frog.png

- ls -l frog.png

- -rwxrw---- 1 harry users 2.7K Jan 4 07:32 frog.png

While it might seem a little strange that the owner of a file can remove the read, write and execute permissions for a file, there are good reasons for doing so. You might have a file that contains data that you don't want to be changed accidentally. While you can remove the permissions, you cannot remove the ability to set the permissions and that means that you retain full control of every file that you own.

Setting Permissions Shorthand

The methods we looked at above to set permissions are easy enough but it can get a little tedious of you have to apply a set of permissions on a regular basis to specific files. You can use shorthand to do this. To understand how the shorthand system works, you must first have a little knowledge on how the numbers system works. The usual numbers system is decimal and it is a base 10 system. This means it has 10 symbol – 0 through 9. There is also the octal system, which has eight symbols – 0 through 7. Now, with three permissions and with each one being on or off, there are 8 combinations. These numbers can also be shown in binary, which has just 2 symbols – 0 and 1. The table below shows how we map from octal to binary:

OCTAL	BINARY
0	000
1	001
2	010
3	011
4	100
5	101
6	110
7	111

Now, all of the octal values can also be represented with 3 binary bits and every combination of 1 and 0 has been included. Now we have 3 permissions and 3 bits. 1 represents on and 0 represents off and, with that, we can use a single octal number to represent a specific set of permissions for a specific set of people. Use 3 numbers and we can set permissions for the owner, the group and others. Let's have a look at an example – don't forget to refer to the above table to see how it all works:

- ls -l frog.png
- -rw-r----x 1 harry users 2.7K Jan 4 07:32 frog.png
- chmod 751 frog.png

- ls -l frog.png
- -rwxr-x--x 1 harry users 2.7K Jan 4 07:32 frog.png
- chmod 240 frog.png
- ls -l frog.png
- --w-r----- 1 harry users 2.7K Jan 4 07:32 frog.png

One convenient method is to remember a common sequence for different file types, i.e. 750 and 755 are used for scripts.

Permissions for Directories

We can use the same permissions for directories but they will behave a little differently:

- r - you have the ability to read the contents of the directory (i.e. do an ls)

- w - you have the ability to write into the directory (i.e. create files and directories)

- x - you have the ability to enter that directory (i.e. cd)

Let's look at some examples of how these work:

- ls testdir
- file1 file2 file3
- chmod 400 testdir
- ls -ld testdir
- -r-------- 1 Simon users 2.7K Jan 4 07:32 testdir
- cd testdir
- cd: testdir: Permission denied

- ls testdir
- file1 file2 file3
- chmod 100 testdir
- ls -ld testdir
- ---x------ 1 Simon users 2.7K Jan 4 07:32 testdir
- cd testdir
- ls testdir
- ls: cannot open directory testdir/: Permission denied

When we ran ls on lines 5 and 14, we also included the option −d, which means directory. Normally, if ls is given an argument that is a directory, it will show the contents for the given directory as an output. However, in this example, what we have asked for is to see the permissions for the given directory and that is what we have been shown.

Permissions can seem somewhat confusing to start with but you just need to remember that these particular ones are for the directory and not the files that are contained in it. Fore example, if you have a directory that you do not have a read permission for, that contains files that do have the read permission for, provided you know that the file is there and you know its name, you are still able to read the files:

- ls -ld testdir
- --x------- 1 Simon users 2.7K Jan 4 07:32 testdir
- cd testdir
- ls testdir
- ls: cannot open directory .: Permission denied

- cat samplefile.txt
- Kyle 20
- Stan 11
- Kenny 37

The Root User

There are just 2 people who can change the file or directory permissions and they are owner for the specific directory or file and root user. This super user has access everything and can do anything. Usually, it would only be a system administrator who could have access to the root account and they would use it to keep the system maintained. Normal users generally only have access to their own files and directories, those located in their home directory, and perhaps a couple of others that are being shared or that they are collaborating on with other users. This is how the stability and the security of the system is maintained.

Basic Security

Your space is your home directory and it is up to you to make sure that it remains as such. Most users tend to give themselves full permissions for read, write and execute on their home directory and will not give permissions to the group or to others. However, everyone has a different set up.

To maintain security, you should refrain from giving write access to your home directory to anyone in the group or others. However, being able to execute without read permissions can be handy at times. This allows others to get to your home directory but they will not be able to see what is contained in it One good example of this is when it is used for personal web pages Systems typically run web servers and each user is given their own bit of space. Commonly, if you were to put a directory into your home directory and call it public_html, the webserver will be able to read the contents and display them. However, because the webserver is a different user, it will not be able to access and read the files. This is where you might want to give execute permissions on the home directory so that the webserver can do its job.

Chapter 10:
The VI Text Editor

In the last chapter, you may remember that we created some blank files. In this chapter, we are going to look at a tool that helps us to put some content into those files and to be able to edit the content as well. Vi is a nice text editor, something different to most of the txt editors you have used in the past. It will take you a while to learn it but, once you have, you will see just how powerful it is.

A Command Line Editor

That is essentially what Vi is – a command line editor. As you know by now, the command line is somewhat different t the Linux GUI. It is just one window where you input text and output text, that is all. Vi works within those strict limitations, making it an extremely powerful editor. It is a plain test editor, similar to TextEdit on the Mac or Notepad on Windows. It is NOT a word processor but it is more powerful than either of the aforementioned built in editors.

You do not need your mouse with Vi, everything in done on the keyboard.

There are two separate modes – Insert (input) and Edit. In the Insert mode, you type in content to go into a file. In Edit, you move around inside the file, and edit the content, like deleting, searching, copying, replacing, saving, etc. One of the most common mistakes that people make is to start inputting commands without being in Edit mode or to start typing in their input without being in Insert mode. Do check before you start. That said, if you do make one of these mistakes, it is easy to recover from it.

To run the Vi text editor, we use one single command line argument, naming the file you want to edit:

- vi <file>

If you don't name a file, you can pen it within Vi but it is actually easier to shut the editor down and start again. Do remember as well that you can use a relative or an absolute path to specify the file name. Right, let's have a look at how this all works.

First of all, with your terminal open, move to the directory that you made called linuxtutorialwork. We want to make some files and we can store them in this to keep them away from everything else you do.

Now we need to edit your first file so type this into the command line:

- vi firstfile

Now, when this command is run, it will open up the file but, if that file does not exit, tit will make it for you before opening it up. When you get into Vi, it may look a little like this (depending on what system you are running):

- ~
- ~
- ~
- ~
- ~

- "firstfile" [New File]

Always start in Edit mode. In this case, we now want to go into Insert mode so press on i. You will from the bottom left corner of your screen when you go into Insert mode.

- ~

- ~

- ~

- ~

- ~

- INSERT --

Type in some text, anything you like and press on Esc. This takes you back into Edit mode.

Saving and Exiting

There are a couple of ways to do this and they all do the same Just choose whichever methis suits you but do make sue that you are in Edit mode first. Again, to make sure, just look at the bottom left corner of the screen. If it is blank, you are ok; if it says Insert you need to get back into Edit mode first. You could just press Esc – if you are already in Edit mode, it won't do anything.

- ZZ (Note

- save and exit

Most of the Vi commands will be executed as soon a key sequence is entered. If a command begins with a col (:) you will need to hit the Enter key for the command to be completed.

Save and exit out of the file that you are in now.

Other Ways To View Files

You can edit files in Vi and you can also view files. However, there are a couple of other commands that are a bit better for doing that. The first is **cat**, short for **concatenate**. It is used to join two files together usually but it can be used to view a file as well:

- cat <file>

Running the cat command with just a single command line argument, will let you see the file content on the screen, followed up by the prompt. If you were to run the cat command with a command line argument, the cursor would move onto the next line but nothing else would happen. If you were to type in some text and then press enter, cat would mirror what you have input onto the screen. You can get out of this by pressing on CTRL+C, which is the Cancel signal in Linux. You can use this to get out of most trouble that you get into in Linux.

- cat firstfile
- here you will see
- whatever content you
- entered in your file

This is a neat command to use if you only have a small file to look at but, when the files are larger, the content will fly across your screen and you will only be able to view the last page. To view larger files, we use a different command called **less**

- less <file>

The less command lets you move through the file contents with the arrow keys. You can forward to the next page with the Space bar or you can press "b" to go back a page. When you are finished, just press "q" to quit it.

Try using both of those commands on the file you created and see how you get on with them.

Navigating A File In Vi

Now, go back to that file and input some more content. While you are in Insert mode, you can use the arrow keys to get around. Type in two more paragraphs and then press Esc so you go back into Edit mode.

The following list are some of the commands that can be used to traverse through a file; have a practice with them and get to grips with how they work:

- Arrow keys - move the cursor around
- j, k, h, l - move the cursor down, up, left and right (similar to the arrow keys)
- ^ (caret) - move cursor to beginning of current line
- $ - move cursor to end of the current line
- nG - move to the nth line (eg 5G moves to 5th line)
- G - move to the last line
- w - move to the beginning of the next word

- nw - move forward n word (eg 2w moves two words forwards)
- b - move to the beginning of the previous word
- nb - move back n word
- { - move backward one paragraph
- } - move forward one paragraph

Deleting content

So we now know how to move around in Vi using one of a number of different options. Deleting works in a similar way and there are a number of different delete commands that you can use to define what you want to delete. The list below shows some of the way to delete – have a practice with them AFTER you have read the next section on how to undo a delete:

- x - delete a single character
- nx - delete n characters (eg 5x deletes five characters)
- dd - delete the current line
- dn - d followed by a movement command. Delete to where the movement command would have taken you. (eg d5w means delete 5 words)

Undoing

It is a fairly easy process to undo a delete in Vi; we just use the letter "u".

- u - Undo the last action (you may keep pressing u to keep undoing)
- U (Note: capital) - Undo all changes to the current line

Taking it Further

Now you know how to insert content, delete it, undo the delete, save it and then exit. This is how to do basic edit work in Vi. While I cannot possibly go into all the details you need to know about Vi, you can take the time out to look into these other features of the text editor:

- copy and paste
- search and replace
- buffers
- markers
- ranges
- settings

All I can say to you now is to have fun; learning Vi will be painful at times but once you have got to grips with it, you won't want to use any other text editor.

Conclusion

Not many years ago, Linux was just a word that computer geeks added to their resumes for it to look better. But nowadays, we can find LINUX in almost all of the data centers and servers in use. The LINUX operating system is pretty straightforward and it is not complex like other operating systems. LINUX is available free of charge in the market which makes it available for everyone who wishes to learn it. Once you install LINUX on your computer, you become a part of the huge LINUX community where you can learn everything about LINUX. In the Linux community, there are people who are willing to help 'newbies' like you.

In this tutorial we have covered the topics like the Linux kernel and shell scripting along with topics like Inter-process Communication and a lot of commands with which you can easily perform most of the simple tasks in Linux. I have also given you a basic overview of using Linux, with plenty of examples to try out for yourselves.

Linux really isn't all that difficult to learn. Once you get into it, you will find that you pick it up quite easily but, and I cannot stress this enough, you must practice. Do not think that, once you have learned something, it will stay with you forever – it won't. And, don't forget, things are changing all the time and advances are constantly being made. If you do not keep at it and you do not keep up with those changes, you will soon fall behind and will find that you have to start all over again.

I want to thank you for downloading my book and I hope you found this tutorial helpful. Please consider leaving a review for me at Amazon.com.